March

Julie Murray

Abdo
MONTHS
Kids

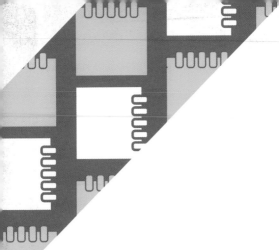

abdopublishing.com

Published by Abdo Kids, a division of ABDO, PO Box 398166, Minneapolis, Minnesota 55439.

Printed in the United States of America, North Mankato, Minnesota.

052017

092017

 THIS BOOK CONTAINS
RECYCLED MATERIALS

Photo Credits: iStock, Shutterstock, ©Korean Resource Center p.22 / CC-BY-SA-2.0

Production Contributors: Teddy Borth, Jennie Forsberg, Grace Hansen

Design Contributors: Christina Doffing, Candice Keimig, Dorothy Toth

Publisher's Cataloging in Publication Data

Names: Murray, Julie, 1969-, author.

Title: March / by Julie Murray.

Description: Minneapolis, Minnesota : Abdo Kids, 2018 | Series: Months |
   Includes bibliographical references and index.

Identifiers: LCCN 2016962332 | ISBN 9781532100178 (lib. bdg.) |
   ISBN 9781532100864 (ebook) | ISBN 9781532101410 (Read-to-me ebook)

Subjects: LCSH: March (Month)--Juvenile literature. | Calendar--Juvenile literature.

Classification: DDC 398/.33--dc23

LC record available at http://lccn.loc.gov/2016962332

Table of Contents

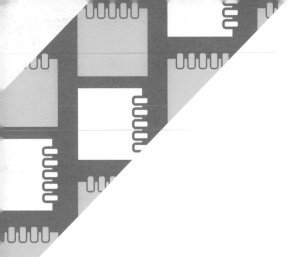

March

There are 12 months in the year.

January

February

March

April

May

June

July

August

September

October

November

December

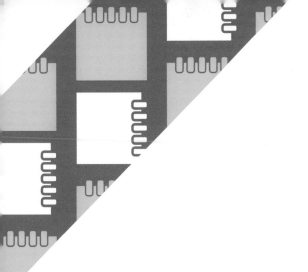

March is the 3rd month.

It has 31 days.

March

1	2	3	4	5	6	7
8	9	10	11	12	13	14
15	16	17	18	19	20	21
22	23	24	25	26	27	28
29	30	31				

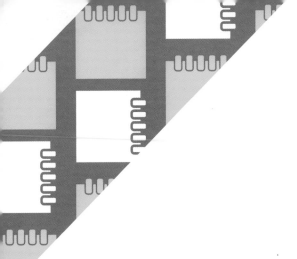

It is Women's History Month.

We celebrate what women have done in the past and today.

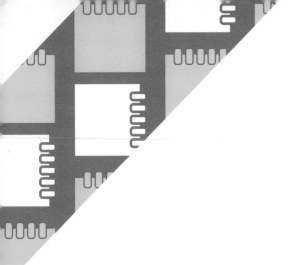

St. Patrick's Day is in March.

It is on the 17th.

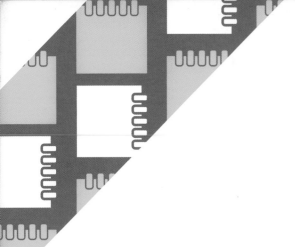

The first day of spring is in March. Lyle plays outside.

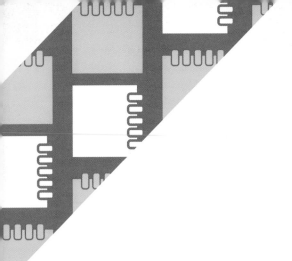

It starts to get warmer.

Snow melts.

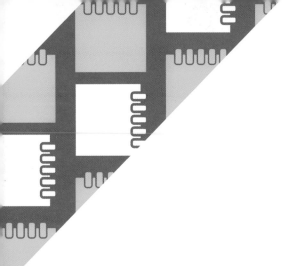

March is messy in Minnesota.

Tina walks in the mud.

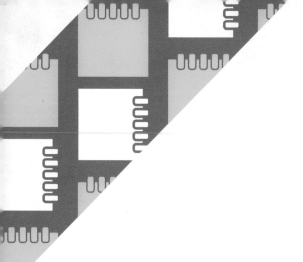

Birds start to sing.

Dana hears the birds.

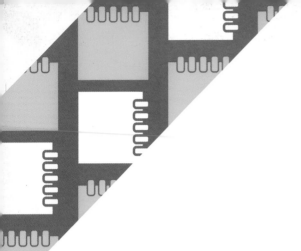

Rob plays at the park.

He loves March!

Fun Days in March

National Pig Day
March 1

Read Across America Day
March 2

Purple Day for Epilepsy
March 26

Cesar Chavez Day
March 31

Glossary

melt
to change from a solid to a liquid state usually by heat.

messy
not clean or tidy.

St. Patrick's Day
a day to celebrate Irish culture with parades, dancing, and more.

23

Index

abdokids.com

Use this code to log on to abdokids.com and access crafts, games, videos, and more!

Abdo Kids Code:
MMK0178